MOOR

FIELD

Written by Berlie Doherty
Illustrated by Sarah Warburton

Collins Educational

An imprint of HarperCollinsPublishers

CHARACTERS

Morgan: guardian of the field

Characters from the past

Cai: a very old man, king of the Druids
Elen: Cai's wife
Olwen: Elen's sister
Young Morgan: Cai's son

Madge: a mystical village woman from 300 years ago
Husband: a village villain
Wife: his wife

Susan: a young peasant woman from 200 years ago
Dan: Susan's young husband, a shepherd
Mother Hobson: Susan's mother
Soldiers: numerous – several with a drum

Characters from the present

Farmer Foxy: a local farmer, rather sly and cunning
Miss Sharp: head of the village school – no nonsense!

Mr Chuzzle: owner of a chocolate factory
Miss Wright: Mr Chuzzle's secretary – has hayfever

Jean: a middle-aged woman
Denis: her husband – a misery!

Mr Walker: a National Park warden
Mrs Cowan: widow of a sheep farmer

SCENE ONE

(The children are already sitting round the sides of the field. In the background, skylarks are singing and there is a running stream. Morgan comes forward from inside the field to the 'For Sale' post, and stands looking out beyond the field and across the valley. Then, noticing the children, he walks round, talking to them.)

Morgan: You've not come to buy my field, have you? Not all of you? No I didn't think you had, really. Not the buying sort, I thought. Not the *field* buying sort, anyway. Makes me nervous though, just to think about it. I'm not sure if I want to part with it for ever. Not going to part with it at all, not if the right person doesn't come along. And what if no-one's interested? That will suit me too – I just want a bit of a rest. It's not that I really want to let it go. And I'll tell you why.

There's more to a field isn't there, than the grass that grows on it, or the stream that waters it? There's more to a field than the old stone wall that bounds it, or the flowers that thrust up in it. What more is there, eh? The people who live and work on it. The animals that graze on it, and stay to hunt there. And deep below the earth, the worms that turn the rich dark soil.

I'd say the field belongs to all of them,

wouldn't you? So who owns the field, eh? Who's got the right to say, 'I'll dig this and I'll plant that and I'll push this in here?' Bah – the things they do to fields!

(Points towards the valley) See this bloke, coming up the hill? I know him – Farmer Foxy. I bet he wants to buy the field. What for though?

SCENE TWO

Farmer Foxy: Morning!

Morgan: Morning, sir! Lovely morning,
Farmer Foxy!

Farmer Foxy: Hmpph. Come up for sale at last,
has it? Morgan's Field. Good. Good. Had me eye
on it for some time, I can tell you. I've made
some plans for this place.

Morgan: *(to children)* What did I tell you!

Farmer Foxy: Oh yes, just right for me, this is –
little bit of water, a few trees for shelter, nice and
flat, good view.

Morgan: Glad you like it.

Farmer Foxy: I do. I've made me mind up. I do like it. I'll take it.

Morgan: Well, just a minute… what was it you were going to grow on it, did you say?

Farmer Foxy: *(laughs)* Grow on it! That's a good one. That's my business. That's my secret. You work it out. What are all the farmers growing now?

Morgan: *(to children)* I don't know? What does he mean? *(to Farmer Foxy)* Same as they've always grown – wheat, maize, barley? Turnips? Flowers, maybe?

Farmer Foxy: You're getting warmer! Bloom like flowers, they do! Great big things… flappy things… great orange and blue and green things!

Morgan: Great big flappy things? How big? *(Stretches out his arms)* This big?

Farmer Foxy: Bigger! Bigger! Bigger!

Morgan: That big! *(to children)* What's he on about? Orange and blue and green things! Flappy things! That big!

Farmer Foxy: Sprouting up like mushrooms all summer long!

Morgan: I give up. I can't fathom that one out. *(to children)* Can you?

Farmer Foxy: Course they can! They've seen 'em.

Morgan: All right then. What do you harvest from it when the summer's over?

Farmer Foxy: Harvest from it? Money, that's what! Money, money, money!

Morgan: I don't know. You've got me guessing.

Farmer Foxy: Ask me another one then.

Morgan: Let's think… ah! Animals! Will you have animals on the field?

Farmer Foxy: I'll say I will! Two-legged ones!

Morgan: *(to children)* Come on, you'll have to help me with this one.

Farmer Foxy: *(to children)* Don't tell him. Let him guess!

Morgan: Well then, in the summer, when they've given you money, money, money, do these two-legged animals eat these great big flappy things?

Farmer Foxy: Eat them? Eat them! They live in them!

(Enter Miss Sharp)

Miss Sharp: And we all know what that means!

Morgan: Do we?

Farmer Foxy: Oh, Lordy! It's Miss Sharp, from the school. Taught half the village, she has. Taught *me* when *I* was young. Still makes me squirm.

Miss Sharp: A camp-site! That's what he wants this field for! Tents, that's what he wants to put up on it! Well, you can't have that. You can't have that.

Morgan: No, I don't suppose I can.

Miss Sharp: Oh, no! Cars… and motorbikes roaring up the lanes.

Morgan: City people. Noisy kids, *(to children)* begging your pardon!

Miss Sharp: Transistor radios blaring all over the hills!

Morgan: Rabbits having heart attacks…

Miss Sharp: Worms punctured with tent pegs…

Morgan: Oh, no! We can't have that!

Miss Sharp: Tents popping up all over the field like coloured blisters! Bony elbows sticking out of them and sweaty socks flapping on the guy ropes!

Morgan: Muddy boots all over the place!

Miss Sharp: One big, boggy mess!

Morgan: I've changed my mind! It's not for sale!

Miss Sharp: Ah! But I have an offer to make…

Farmer Foxy: She would… the old baggage!

Miss Sharp: Quiet, Foxy.

Farmer Foxy: Yes, Miss. Sorry, Miss.

Miss Sharp: On behalf of my school. It's most important, d'you see, for my children to have a playing field.

Farmer Foxy: A playing field! With all this countryside sticking up their noses. I'd say it was more important for city kids to have a holiday out here!

Miss Sharp: Don't interrupt, Foxy!

Farmer Foxy: No, Miss. Sorry, Miss.

Miss Sharp: Every time they kick a ball it goes through the church window. Our school yard isn't big enough for them to turn a skipping rope in, d'you see. They need somewhere to run and stretch their little legs…

10

Farmer Foxy: They'd break their little legs on all these stones.

Morgan: These stones…

Miss Sharp: Oh, we'll soon get rid of all this lot…

Farmer Foxy: Tell her about these stones. Tell her they've been here hundreds and hundreds of years! *I* wouldn't shift 'em. *I'd* leave 'em be. It's a tourist attraction, this place is. Old as the hills, these stones. Tell her!

Miss Sharp: What's he whispering to you about? He can't offer you more than I can, you know! I've got the Education Committee on my side. Foxy, keep your nose where it ought to be, in the middle of your face. Be off with you!

Farmer Foxy: Yes, Miss. *(to Morgan)* Tell her! *(goes)*

Miss Sharp: Well?

Morgan: People used to live here, on this field, hundreds and hundreds of years ago. People died here, and were buried… and have slept long since in the cool earth. I don't like the thought of letting children loose here, screaming, shouting and running around, kicking up the dust of centuries: raising the dead with their hullabaloo!

Miss Sharp: And what, may I ask, did children do all those years ago when they lived here, if what you say is true? Did they never make a sound? *(goes)*

Morgan: Of course they did. And I can hear them now… their voices laughing. Calling to each other on the wind… voices echoing in these dear, dark hills. Dead and laid to rest so many years ago!

Let me rest, too!

Let me tell you about the very first people who ever came to live on this field – over two thousand years ago. They were Druids, a wise and mystic people: they loved peace, not war; they fled from barbarous bands. They loved beauty, not wealth, and looked to the land for their livelihood. They came from the West in search of fruitful earth, but they would not rest until they had found a land that they could love. They struggled for many weeks across the mountains; they suffered the iced bite of the wind from the North and the mist that wrapped itself around their eyes. At last they came down from the dark moors towards this field. And as they came down, the wind limped away from them. The mist like an old, grey ghost drifted back to the hills. The sun blessed their weary limbs.

(Cai*, Elen and Olwen come into the field.)

Leading them was Cai, Druid King, a good and holy man, and very old. With him, his wife Elen, weak from much walking. Olwen, her sister, and Morgan, their son, driving their poor animals.

(Young Morgan enters the field.)

* Cai pronounced Kye

SCENE THREE

Young Morgan: Father! Wait!

Elen: Yes, Cai, we must rest here. I can't go any further. And besides, our people are miles behind us. Look where they are still, struggling down from the misty hills. I think we should wait here for them.

Cai: There's no time to wait. No time to stop, I tell you. My time is short enough.

Olwen: It would be good to rest here. It's so sheltered.

Cai: My time is short enough. I dare not rest until I have found the right place for us to live in.

Elen: But we've been walking now for weeks. Is there to be no rest for us, ever?

Young Morgan: Father! Why don't we stop here?

Cai: I've told you…

Young Morgan: Not to rest, Father! To live!

Cai: To live! Here! You think this is where our journey ends? Look at it.

14

Young Morgan: This has to be the place we're searching for. Mountains – fold on fold of mountains behind us to give us shelter from the cold fingers of the wind. Bushes, bright with berries – there's food for us. Water here, to drink from and to bathe in. Huge stones, cast down from these mountains, for us to build our houses with, to make shelters for our animals, to wall us in. And below us… look! This rich valley for us to grow our crops, and to see from far away the approach of enemies.

Elen: Listen to the boy. He's right, Cai. This is a place of peace.

Cai: It is a good place. But… we must be sure…

Young Morgan: I am sure. I know it. It's right for us, this field.

Olwen: Please, Cai. I feel it too. This should be our home.

Cai: You are right. We belong here. I see this field is good for you, Morgan. And Elen. And Olwen. May it always be good for our people, and for all who choose to live here. Come. Let us bless this earth.

(From the centre of the field he scoops a handful of earth and gives some to all of them. They each take a corner of the field and come together again to the centre while they chant:)

Cai: May this good earth

Elen: This earth

Young Morgan: Bring riches

Olwen: Riches

Cai: To our holy people.

Elen: May the good

Young Morgan: Good sun

Olwen: Provide for us.

Cai: Let there be

Elen: Love

Young Morgan: In life,

Olwen: And peace

Cai: Peace

Elen: In death

Young Morgan: Upon this

Olwen: Earth,

Cai: This chosen

All: Upon this chosen earth.

(They embrace each other.)

Elen: There now! I feel my weariness draining away from me!

Olwen: Me, too! I feel a new life in me! I'm ready to start building our homes now!

Young Morgan: Minutes ago you could hardly walk! Look, I'll move these. You bring across those smaller stones. Roll them.

Olwen: Look at the energy of the boy! He'd do this all on his own, if he could.

Elen: But see how frail his father has become. It's as if Morgan is drawing all his strength from Cai.

Olwen: Yes, Cai's very weak. He should rest now and leave it to the boy. We need more help.

Elen: Let's bring our brothers and sisters down from the hills. They'll come more quickly when they know the field is found.

Olwen: And the children! They'll love it here. Wait till they see the lovely home Cai has chosen for them.

Elen: Not Cai! Morgan chose it!

(Elen and Olwen go.)

Cai: I've no strength left to help you. I'm an old man, fit to die, and ready.

Young Morgan: No, father…

Cai: I see this as a fit resting place. I'm content to end my days here. And I'm content for our people to start a new life here. But not with me. It will be for you, Morgan, to lead them now. If this is to be your home, so be it. It is good, yes. I see that it is good. A fit dwelling place for you and all your people. We'll call it 'Morgan's Field'. But you must always guard it well.

Young Morgan: I will, father. I'll guard it with my life.

Cai: And beyond your lifetime, too. I tell you, you will never rest. This is chosen land, and you are its chosen protector. Be sure you know what that means. Let no-one take this field from you who does not love it as you do. That you must promise me, my son.

Young Morgan: I do… of course I do.

(Cai leads him to the centre of the field and Young Morgan kneels. Cai stoops, takes a handful of earth and holds it out to Young Morgan as he speaks:)

Cai: May this earth
     Bring riches
     To your people.
     May the sun
     Provide for you.
     Let there be no hatred
     Upon your earth.
     Let there be love in life.

(He gestures to Young Morgan to take the earth and stand while he kneels in his place. Young Morgan holds up the earth and sprinkles it on his father.)

Cai: *(prompts him)* And peace…

Young Morgan: And peace
               In death.

(Elen and Olwen have come and are standing at the edge of the field.)

All: Upon this chosen earth.

(Cai and Young Morgan embrace.)

Cai: And now I take my leave of you.

Young Morgan: Father…

Elen: Cai, are you well?

Cai: I'll never be as well as this again. Dear wife. Help me to the far corner of the field. Your home is here. My journey is now ended. I can rest.

(Elen helps Cai walk away.)

Morgan: *(to children as he moves across the field)* And that was the gift – and the burden – that my father left me with. And it perplexed me, I can tell you, to know how I could keep my promise to him. 'You will never rest,' he said. How right he was.

We built eight stone houses here *(pointing)*, and here, for our people. This wall here *(pointing)* sheltered our animals. We lived in this place for years and years, and one by one my people died. Their bodies were given to this far corner of the field – that's where they lie. And then I knew the power of my father's word. No rest for me – protector of this field – for ever! 'Let no-one take this field from you who does not love it as you do.'

But here are more buyers. Watch them. Will one of them buy it?

SCENE FOUR

Mr Chuzzle: Well, well, now what d'you think of this, Miss Wright? Hmm? What d'you think of this?

Miss Wright: (*sneezes*) Very nice, Mr Chuzzle.

Mr Chuzzle: I can see it all! Little tubs of geraniums round the gate. A little pool in the centre, with a little fountain, Miss Wright, splashing up into the sky!

Miss Wright: It won't hide the factory, Mr Chuzzle…

Mr Chuzzle: Now now, Miss Wright, our little factory brings no offence to anyone… no offence… work for the local people, now that's not to be sniffed at, is it? And untold happiness to children everywhere! We don't want to hide our factory! We want to show it off! We're proud of it! CHUZZLE'S CHOCOLATES, in big blue letters against the hills for everyone to see! Little blue Chuzzle Chocolate vans buzzing up and down the lanes, up and down, with their cargoes of treasures. Ah!

We'll bring the bulldozers in on Monday. We'll start in that far corner of the field. Write that down, Miss Wright.

Miss Wright: *(sneezes)* I can't, Mr Chuzzle.

Mr Chuzzle: Come, come, an order is an order… write it down!

Miss Wright: I can't see, Mr Chuzzle… my eyes are streaming that much!

Mr Chuzzle: My dear, I know. It is a moving thought. It is a moving thought. A new Chuzzle factory opening up. Every time I open up a new factory, I have to admit it, Miss Wright, I get a lump in my throat… and yes, I weep a little tear or two! What a soft-centred little man I am!

Miss Wright: It's not emotion… it's sneezes! Fresh air always makes me sneeze. I don't like it here one bit.

Morgan: Neither do I! A factory – here – sending smoke and sticky smells all over the valley! Big blue letters in the sky! Little blue vans all over the place! Is that want I want? And busloads of kids no doubt – *(to children)* begging your pardon – on school visits, pockets bulging with bags of chocolate brazils… I'll not have it.

Mr Chuzzle: School visits… what a good idea, Miss Wright. Write it down.

(Morgan pulls down the sign and charges at them with it.)

Morgan: Not in my field you don't…

Miss Wright: Oh, Mr Chuzzle!

Mr Chuzzle: Go and sit in the car, Miss Wright, and blow your nose. I'll deal with this. *(Miss Wright goes.)* Now, my dear good sir, I believe you're the gentleman who is selling this field. I can see that you're a reasonable man. Let's talk business, shall we? *(takes a bag from his pocket)* Have a chocolate… go on… spoil yourself!

(Morgan takes one and flings it to the ground.)

Morgan: Bah! Chocolate! Hate the stuff!

(Chuzzle picks it up and puts it in his bag.)

Mr Chuzzle: Don't leave litter, dear sir! Can't have that in our nice clean countryside, can we? Have you had many buyers… you know… interested in this field of yours?

Morgan: Hmmpph. Maybe I have, and maybe I haven't.

Mr Chuzzle: Because, let me make it quite plain to you… *(draws fistfuls of notes from his pockets)* …whatever they've offered you, I can offer more. *(to children)* Is that what he's after? More and more and more. *(to Morgan)* You'll be a very wealthy man. Think of it. Everyone will be better off. There'll be work in the valley for all those people who haven't got jobs to go to. There'll be chocolates for all those children who've never tasted Chuzzle's Chocolates before. And children love chocolates, don't they? *(to children)* Dear little things! *(to Morgan)* How much did you want for it, did you say?

Morgan: I didn't.

Mr Chuzzle: I'll pay you twice as much. I'll pay you double what anyone else wants to pay. Remember that. Remember that. (*As he goes out he offers chocolates from his bag to some of the children.*)

Morgan: Bah! Chocolates! They rot your teeth! Money! Is that what I want for my field? Money? Bah! (*He replaces the post.*) I knew it was a mistake, I knew I'd get all sorts of riff-raff in looking at the place once I'd put it up for sale. Better to leave it to chance till someone just wanders in and decides they'd like to stay. That's what I did when I chose this field. People come and people go, and some have made their homes here for a while, but left no trace. Like Madge there. (*turns towards the field as Madge comes into the centre of it, singing and picking flowers*) How many years ago, Madge? Five hundred? You loved my field.

SCENE FIVE

Morgan: *(to children)* One bright day, when the sky was as blue as it could ever be and the old lark was out of sight in it somewhere, singing and singing till you would have thought its body would have burst with song, there came another song, an up-and-down chanting sort of song, and a scraping at the earth in the very centre of my field. 'Who's that?' I shouted. 'Who's making noises in my field?'

Madge: *(sings)*
> Celandine yellow and Herb
>   Robert pink
> And campion and toadflax as
>   red as the dawn
> And bluebells and ladysmock
> Water forget-me-not,
> Dogrose and gentian and flower
>   on the thorn...

Morgan: Madge! Singing her sweet song, looking for new bright flowers in the grass.

Madge: Do you like my pretties? I found them! They're mine! Do you like my precious little jewels? Shan't have them! Look, sir, how they glow; red and white and blue and gold! Smell this spearmint, sir... crumble it in your fingers, sir. Ah… good is it? Smell the wild garlic when the morning's damp, sir… and honeysuckle, when the sun's too hot to breathe. But see the bright jewels in the grass, sir… my pretties! Don't tell… don't tell them where my jewels is hid! My speedwell, and my wild pansies, and look, sir… foxgloves! Don't tell them!

Morgan: Tell who, Madge?

Madge: The people in the village, sir… they're looking for Madge's jewels. But it's my secret… ah! It's Madge's secret. Nobody's going to take Madge's pretties from her.

Morgan: They won't, Madge. Don't you worry. Your pretty jewels are safe here in my field.

Madge: Ah, sir… nothing's safe! I know where *your* jewels is hid and buried, sir, over in that far corner of the field. White bones, sir, in the cold dark soil. I know that, sir… ah… I know it. And I see a time when men will want to come and dig up your precious jewels, sir… I see a time when men will want to come with big monsters to chew and churn this earth up. People used to live here and children play here sir… round these boulders. These were houses once… ah, I know that. And I see a time when men will want to break up these boulders, sir, these ancient houses, sir, and scatter them like broken beads. I see it, sir, I see it. Madge sees it all.

Morgan: What else do you know, Madge? What can you hear?

Madge: I can hear sheep's voices, sir, across all time. I can hear the wind from the mountains, like a children's song. I can hear the Druid chant, sir… 'Let there be no hatred upon this earth, nor in it.' And drums, sir, drums like heavy footsteps marching. And digging! I can hear digging in your field. My bright buttercups, and my pretty primroses that bring the springtime on.They want them, sir! They plague me, oh they plague me! They drive me from my home!

Morgan: Because you can see things Madge? They're frightened of you!

Madge: I don't know, sir, but I'm afeard of them right enough! I'm afeard they'll take my jewels from me.

Morgan: You must stay here then, Madge. Would you like that?

Madge: Live here, sir… with my flowers? Oh yes, sir… Madge loves your field.

Morgan: All summer long Madge tended her pretty jewels as she called them. She built herself a hovel by the stream... Then one night, when those dark hills were blacker than the sky, two villagers crept into the field.

(Morgan and Madge go as if to sleep at opposite ends of the field while the two villagers creep with their spades into the field...)

Husband: Shh!

Wife: Shh!

Husband: I think the old hag sleeps over there!

Wife: She snores like a toad!

Husband: Let's dig then.

Wife: Where?

Husband: Where?

Wife: Where's she buried them?

Husband: In the earth, fool!

Wife: Shh. There's a lot of earth in a field, husband.

Husband: Then we'll dig till dawn.

(They dig frantically from one end of the field to another.)

(Morgan stands.)

Morgan: What are you doing in my field?

Husband: Shh!

Wife: Don't wake the hag up!

Husband: We're digging…

Morgan: I can see that…

Wife: For her jewels…

Husband: Buried in the earth… that's what she told us…

Wife: But we'll find them…

Husband: We'll find them…

Wife: We'll share them with you, if you help us…

Husband: What does she want jewels for?

Wife: At her age.

Husband: Ugly old bag!

Wife: Shh!

Husband: Don't just stand there.

Wife: Get digging…

Husband: Get on with it!

Morgan: Get out of my field!

Wife: Shh!

(Madge stands and runs to them.)

Madge: My jewels! My pretty jewels. You've dug up all my jewels, Madge's precious pretty jewels.

Husband: Where?

Wife: Where?

Husband: They're not jewels… grass… herbs… common wild flowers…

Wife: Buttercups and cowslips…

Madge: My pretties!

Morgan: GET OUT!

Husband: See what she's done, wife…

Wife: I do see… she's turned her jewels…

Husband: …into plants!

Wife: Mean thing.

Husband: So we wouldn't have them…

Wife: She's a witch!

Husband: I told you that before.

Wife: She's a witch. A witch.

Husband: Turns rubies into poppies.

Wife: Gold into buttercups…

Husband: Turns silver into cowslips. Witch… she's a witch.

(Madge takes to her heels and runs from the field and they chase her, followed by Morgan.)

Morgan: I never let them near my field again, I can tell you. Poor Madge slipped back when she dared, to make her flowers grow again. Poor old Madge. She loved my field. And the flowers did grow again, and the grasses, where those greedy villagers had dug, and it was as if they had never been. Peace came to my field again. But not to me. Will I ever rest? Will no-one come who loves my field and can care for it as I do?

What do you think I should do? Should I let those tents grow here, alongside Madge's pretties? What would she say, d'you think? Or should I let the village children play here, where all my people's children played all those hundreds of years ago? Would they wake from their long sleep, eh, and join them in their games?

And what about that strawberry cream fellow... that hazelnut cluster... what's his name? Chuzzle! Children don't like chocolates that much do they, to grow them in a field? Do they? I don't know. What shall I do?

SCENE SIX

Jean: *(off)* Denis!

Morgan: More of them!

Denis: *(off)* It's stuck, I tell you. Wheels are stuck in the ditch!

Jean: *(coming on)* Hurry up, Denis! Never mind the old car. I can't wait to see it. Oh, look!

Morgan: Townies, you can tell.

Jean: Denis! Come on, quick.

Denis: What's the rush? *(coming on)* It's not going to fly away is it?

Jean: Well? What do you think?

Denis: Looks like any other field to me.

Morgan: Did you hear that? Cheek!

Jean: It's a beautiful field. Lovely dark mountains behind – look at the shadows of the clouds moving across... and heather on the slopes! Oh, look over there... a stream, Denis, there's a stream in the field!

Denis: And midges, I'll bet.

Jean: And what a lovely view, right across the valley. See the patterns the fields make – and the sun on the river, right down there!

Denis: Too exposed! You'd lose your washing off the line.

Morgan: Washing! Don't like the sound of that.

Jean: And every evening we could sit and watch the sunset.

Denis: You're facing the wrong way... sun sets over there.

Morgan: Right old misery guts. She's got the right idea, though.

Jean: But, Denis. Denis. You promised me – you said, 'I'll build you a dream house in the place you love most' – and this is it. I love this place. I do.

Madge: *(from field)* Don't listen to her, Morgan! They want to dig our jewels up...

Denis: We'd have to start from scratch... dig up half the field.

Madge: Our jewels, Morgan! Our pretties!

Morgan: Here we go. Builders, lorries and cement mixers, dust everywhere, shouting and banging – scaring the rabbits and the skylarks off for good... I knew there'd be a catch in it, if she liked it. But he's bound to make her change her mind... I mean, it's miles from anywhere.

Denis: It's miles from anywhere, love.

Jean: Forty-five minutes drive away from the city. That's nothing.

Morgan: Too far.

Denis: Too far.

Jean: But it's worth it for the peace! Listen! Just listen!

Denis: Can't hear a thing.

Jean: Exactly. There isn't a sound to break the silence.

Morgan: Just wait for the dawn chorus.

Denis: Just wait for the dawn chorus.

Jean: Country sounds – the sounds of nature.

Denis: Well I'd rather listen to the sounds of a traffic jam. Come on Jean! *(going)*

Jean: Please, Denis!

Denis: I'll come back later with some earplugs. And some wellies. Now come and help me shift this car from the ditch.

(They go.)

Morgan: That was a near thing, I must say. Nearly fell for all her pretty talk, but I can't stand the likes of him. Moaning. Picking faults. Not good enough for him, was it? Well, *he* wasn't good enough for *it*! And yet… she wanted this field because she loved it. Maybe I should talk to them again. Excuse me, sir – just a minute!

(Denis comes in.)

Denis: What's this then? Ah, wanting me to make an offer, are you?

Morgan: Well, we haven't really talked it over, have we, sir?

Denis: No, and I haven't thought it over yet, that's why. I haven't made my mind up.

Morgan: It's just that… the lady seems quite keen…

Denis: That's true enough. She's set her heart on the place. But… well, I'm not sure…

Morgan: I want to tell you about another time, when a young couple just like you came to set up house here – would you mind, sir…

(Morgan opens the gate and draws Denis into the field.)

Denis: What's this? What do you want me to do?

Morgan: Come in, sir, if you will.

(Denis enters field.)

Morgan: I want you to watch something that happened here two hundred years ago.

(Jean comes in.)

Jean: What's happening, Denis? Can we have the field?

Morgan: Come in, that's right. And just stand there. Just watch with me. There's Dan and Susan. Watch them.

SCENE SEVEN

(Dan comes across the field to the boulders and Susan stands at the edge of the field while Morgan is talking.)

Morgan: I saw Dan sliding in one night when the moon was low. He crept like a cat across the field and tucked himself against the flattened wall of my old house. That's Susan, his young wife.

Susan: *(sings)*
> On the day that I was married
> And in my marriage bed
> A bold sea captain he came to me
> And he stood at my bed's head,
> Crying, 'Arise, arise young married man
> And come along with me
> To the low low lands of Holland
> To fight the enemy.'*

Morgan: I went up to the lad, but quiet-like. I could see he was trying to hide himself, but as soon as he heard me coming he jumped up like a rabbit and would have been off and out of the field if I hadn't stopped him. *(goes up to him)* There he goes! *(holds him)* Keep still now! Stay!

Dan: Let go! Leave me be, I say! Let go!

* The music to this song is found on page 64.

Morgan: I don't mean you any harm. I won't hurt you. Right. I just want to know who you are and what you're doing here.

Dan: Nothing… I'm doing nothing, I promise you. Let me go.

Morgan: Now I know you! Let's look at you. You're the shepherd boy from over the hill. I've seen you many a time with your flock along the top there.

Dan: Yes, sir. Dan's my name. But I don't know you.

Morgan: Let's say I'm a shepherd, too. I've watched sheep cropping these hills for years and years and years. But Dan… why are you hiding?

Dan: Wasn't hiding, sir.

Morgan: Have you done something wrong?

Dan: No I haven't. I'm a good boy, sir, and I've never lost a ewe nor a lamb, sir, not in snow, nor in fog. But they're after me, sir.

Morgan: Who are Dan? The sheep!

Dan: The king's men! Looking for soldiers, sir, marching all the young men down from the fields and the hills, marching them across ENGLAND, sir! And then they're taking them across the sea to a place called Holland. It's in the name of war, they say.

Morgan: And you're not proud to go then, Dan – to be called to fight for your king and for your country?

Dan: That I'm not, sir! What do I want with fighting – what do I want with war? What do I want with my king – I don't know him and he don't know me, so why should I go and die for him? I'm a shepherd, not a soldier. I'll die a shepherd, too. I know these hills, I love these hills, sir. This is where I want to be.

Susan: Dan! Dan! Do you hear them?

Dan: And besides, there's Susan.

Morgan: Ah. Susan. Your sweetheart.

Dan: My wife, sir. I married her today. But she's that frightened, sir, that the king's men will come and take me from her. Watching for them, listening for them, for the rat-tat-tat of their drums and toot-tootle-too of their horns to tell us that they've come for the young men of the valley.

Morgan: Look, Dan. Hide in this shelter. They'll never find you here. And when they've gone, let you and Susan build your home here.

Dan: Sir, we love this place.

Morgan: I know, Dan. You shall have it. And... I shall rest. *(comes back to the edge of the field and addresses Denis and Jean)* How wrong I was to take my rest that night! I stretched myself under this old stone wall and slept, knowing that Dan and Susan loved their home here. And while I slept... *(Lies down. Distant sound of drums)*

(Susan, still on edge of field, sings…)

Susan: I held my love all in my arms
              Still thinking he might stay
              But the captain he gave another order
              He was forced to march away
              Saying there's many a blithe young
                married man
              This night must go with me
              To the low low lands of Holland
              To fight the enemy.

(Drums come closer. Soldiers surround the field beating their drums.)

(Mother Hobson runs into the field and back to Susan.)

Susan: Mother!

Mother Hobson: Where is he? Where've you hidden him?

Susan: He's sleeping, Mother. Don't waken him. Don't let the soldiers hear you.

Mother Hobson: The soldiers. The soldiers. We're all lost child. We're all lost now. Your father's gone with them tonight.

Susan: My father?

Mother Hobson: Gone to be a soldier, with the other men! Gone to save us from the enemy! Where's your man then?

Susan: I've told you... he's asleep.

Mother Hobson: Then rouse him.

Susan: Leave him, Mother! Oh, I can hear them coming nearer!

Mother Hobson: Out mole! Out rat! Out you skulking coward!

Dan: What? Have they come? Oh, good Mother Hobson, I thought you was the soldiers coming for me!

Mother Hobson: Stand yourself straight. What sort of a man are you, eh, to marry my daughter in the day and let her stand guard for you at night? What sort of a man are you to say you love your country and your wife, and not to fight to save them? Leave it to the others would you! What sort of a man is that?

Dan: I don't know, I don't know, Mother Hobson. All I know is that I'm not a fighting man...

Mother Hobson: Neither was my husband, but he's gone with them...

Susan: Leave him, Mother... It's for *my* sake he's hiding.

Mother Hobson: Why should he be saved? They took my man – let them take yours, too!

(Soldiers begin to march into the field, still drumming.)

Susan: They're coming... oh they're coming!

Dan: What shall I do, Susan?

Susan: Run, Dan! Run! Run for your life!

Mother Hobson: Go to them, I say. Give yourself to them like a proper man.

Susan: They're here!

Mother Hobson: Go to them.

Susan: Save yourself.

Dan: Goodbye, Susan. I'll come back to you. Even if they take me I'll come back to you. *(Goes. The soldiers follow him.)*

Susan: Oh run, Dan.

Mother Hobson: If you run they'll shoot.

Dan: *(off)* Goodbye, Susan…

(Drums take up and get louder and louder. They end on a single beat, like a rifle shot. Susan screams and follows with Mother Hobson.)

(Jean and Denis hold hands and walk away, sad.)

SCENE EIGHT

(Morgan sits up, rubs his eyes, and stretches. As he stands Mr Walker comes up to the gate.)

Mr Walker: Morning!

Morgan: Oh! Morning! Morning to you, sir!

Mr Walker: I'm sorry... didn't mean to startle you.

Morgan: Didn't see you coming! I was miles away!

Mr Walker: I've just heard this field is up for sale. I'm very interested.

Morgan: You're not the only one... there was a young couple here just now as a matter of fact: very keen but... looks as if they've gone. Aye, there's been a few after it today.

Mr Walker: That doesn't surprise me. It's gone then, has it?

Morgan: No. No, not yet. Not made my mind up yet.

Mr Walker: I've always been fond of this place. I've passed through many a time on my way to the top. Ah! Morgan's Field.

Morgan: Aye, that's what the locals call it. I've heard it was called Coward's Field for a time. They say a young lad hid here because he didn't want to fight for his king and country. Going back near three hundred years, that would be. They reckon he was shot, this lad, running away from the soldiers here.

Mr Walker: Funny how these tales linger on. But I've often felt that about the field, as if it has some stories to tell, you know, from the past.

Morgan: Oh, it has that. Aye, it has that.

Mr Walker: Yes. I've always liked this field.

(Mrs Cowan runs in.)

Mrs Cowan: I'm not too late, am I? Not sold it yet, have you? My golly, my gosh, it's run about, up and down, morning noon and night. How you two men have time to stand about gossiping about nothing I really don't know, I just don't know. Now I'll have this field off you, if it's yours to have off of, then I shall have to skip back to my hens, and then there's those cows that need milking. Morning, noon and night, it's never stop I tell you. I shall never catch up with myself trailing up here.

Morgan: *(to children)* Mrs Cowan… Farmer Cowan's widow.

Mrs Cowan: I'll bring my sheep in tomorrow morning. Early light, mind – tomorrow's market day.

Mr Walker: One minute, Mrs Cowan… I think I may be buying this field.

Mrs Cowan: Too late! Too late! I've just bought it! Dear, dear, who else should buy a field but a farmer?

Mr Walker: Well… I think my claim is a pretty strong one, too.

Morgan: I've seen you around, now come to think about it. Mending walls and fences… putting stepping stones in streams.

Mr Walker: That's right. Walker, my name is. I work here for the National Park. I'm a warden.

Mrs Cowan: That lot! Can't abide you, National Park! Encouraging people to come out here, tramping around across the hills as if they own the place! What right have they got to fresh air? They chose to live in the city – that's their own fault.

Mr Walker: Oh, I think there's plenty of room to share out here, don't you?

Mrs Cowan: It's what they do when they get here as troubles me – barging through crops, scaring sheep, knocking walls down...

Mr Walker: That's why we want to buy it! All we want to do is put a footpath through it, leading visitors up to the moors. Then they won't go wandering off where you don't want them to be.

Morgan: Well, that's a new one. Put a footpath through it, did you say? You mean you don't want to go digging things up and shoving this here and that there...

Mr Walker: That's the last thing we want to do. Oh, no, we want to keep this field exactly as it is so everyone can enjoy it.

Mrs Cowan: They don't know how to enjoy it, city folk. There'll be all sorts up here, picking the flowers, chucking them down again, letting them die… I hate to see that.

Mr Walker: We wouldn't touch the flowers. We ask people to leave things as they find them. You wouldn't find many coming up this far, except the real country lovers.

Morgan: That's true enough. Never see a soul from one day's end to the next, save for the rabbits and the odd mountain hare.

Mrs Cowan: Now – you'll have sheep for company if you let me have the field!

Morgan: It's not company I'm after. It's peace.

Mr Walker: Well then, it's as good as mine. There'll be no changes here, I can promise you that, if we buy it. And nobody building on it. Ever.

Mrs Cowan: What would your people think of sheep grazing on it, eh, Mr Walker? What harm would that do?

Mr Walker: None at all, as far as I can see!

Mrs Cowan: There you are! What else should a field be used for, for goodness sake? It's the most natural thing in the world.

Morgan: Well. *He* makes sense, and *she* makes sense. What do I do?

Mrs Cowan: Why don't we both use it then? You buy it, and I can rent it off you...

Mr Walker: You keep your sheep here...

Mrs Cowan: And you put your footpath through!

Morgan: Hang on a minute! Not so fast –

Mrs Cowan: That's settled then.
Everyone's satisfied!

Morgan: Are they? I want to think about this... there's those tents to think of – people having holidays here...And the school children... nowhere else for them to play...

Mrs Cowan: And you'd keep everyone out at lambing time, wouldn't you?

Morgan: And all those chocolates… they've got to be made somewhere. Oh dear… and Denis and Jean… she'd be so happy here… I don't know… I don't know what to think…

(Unseen by Mr Walker and Mrs Cowan, Morgan takes the sign down and goes slowly to the centre of the field. He scoops up some earth and carries it over to the far corner where his ancestors are buried. He lies down as if to sleep by the sign.)

Mrs Cowan: It'll be just the same as it's always been. It's nice to think that. Grass and flowers growing round these old boulders. Insects droning over it. Skylark up there, singing the song it's sung for centuries. No need for…

Mr Walker: …anything to change. No need for anyone to come here, except those who love it…

Mrs Cowan: Why, it's only an old field, fit for sheep to graze on…

Mr Walker: I don't know Mrs Cowan. I think there's something special about this one.

Mrs Cowan: Well, can't stand here all day. It's a fair scramble from my farm. I'm not looking forward to charging up and down here all the time, that's the only trouble. Now, I could ask that old bloke to keep an eye on my sheep for me...Well! I don't know! He's gone!

Mr Walker: And so's the sign!

Mrs Cowan: Fancy walking off like that!

Mr Walker: How come we didn't see him go?

Mrs Cowan: What does that mean then? I bet he's changed his mind... I bet he's decided not to sell it after all. And I've trailed up here...

Mr Walker: Perhaps he's made his mind up... decided who to sell it to? Come on Mrs Cowan. Let's go. I'll give you a lift back to your farm. We'll leave this field in peace, shall we? We'll leave it as it is.

(Larksong)

(Silence)

End

The Lowlands of Holland

Traditional

1. On the day that I was mar - ried And in my mar - riage bed A bold sea cap - tain he came to me And he stood at my bed's head, Crying, 'A - rise, a - rise young mar - ried man And come a - long with me To the low low lands of Hol - land To fight the en - e - my.'

2. I held my love all in my arms Still think - ing he might stay But the cap - tain he gave an - other or - der He was forced to march a - way Saying there's ma - ny a blithe young mar - ried man This night must go with me To the low low lands of Hol - land To fight the en - e - my.'